INFORMATION LIBRARY

ANIMAL LIFE

Steve Pollock

Gareth Stevens Children's Books
MILWAUKEE

For a free color catalog describing Gareth Stevens' list of high-quality children's books call 1-800-341-3569

Library of Congress Cataloging-in-Publication Data
Pollock, Steve (Stephen Thomas)
     Animal life / by Steve Pollock.
          p. cm. — (Gareth Stevens information library)

     Includes index.
     Summary: A survey of the characteristics, habits, and natural environment of animals
from all over the world. Also introduces the scientific grouping and classification of animal life.
     ISBN 0-8368-0003-6
     1. Animals—Juvenile literature. 2. Zoology—Classification—Juvenile literature. I. Title. II. Series.
     [DNLM: 1. Animals. 2. Zoology—Classification.]
QL49.P742   1989
591—dc20   89-11367

North American edition first published in 1990 by
Gareth Stevens, Inc.
RiverCenter Building, Suite 201
1555 North RiverCenter Drive
Milwaukee, Wisconsin 53212, USA

Photographic credits: Bruce Coleman, pp. 26, 36 (right), 37, 52; Frank Lane, pp. 15, 18 (right), 25,
30, 32-34, 36 (left), 38, 40, 43, 45, 46, 48, 49, 53, 55-59; Natural Science Photos, pp. 18 (left), 19
(right); NHPA, p. 27; Oxford Scientific Films, pp. 31, 39; Planet Earth, pp. 9, 58

Illustrated by Adam Abel, Teresa O'Brien, Eric Robson, Roger Walker, and Lorna Turpin

Series editor: Neil Champion
Editor (US): Mark Sachner
Research editor: Scott Enk
Educational consultant: Dr. Alistair Ross
Editorial consultant: Neil Morris
Design: Groom and Pickerill
Cover design: Kate Kriege
Picture research and art editing: Ann Usborne
Specialist consultant: the late Dr. Gwynne Vevers

Printed in the United States of America

1 2 3 4 5 6 7 8 9 96 95 94 93 92 91 90

Contents

913268

1: ANIMAL LIFE

The Animal Kingdom

Animals are living things that share many features and traits. All animals must eat and breathe, and most animals move. After they eat or drink, all animals make waste materials which they must remove. Animals find out about their surroundings by using their senses: sight, hearing, touch, taste, and smell. All animals eventually die, so only by reproducing can they make sure their own kind continues.

Animals everywhere

Animals can be found almost anywhere, from high mountains to the deepest, darkest depths of the oceans. They live in the air, in trees, and underground. There are few places where animals cannot live.

Every animal is adapted to a particular way of life. A penguin is adapted to life in the water. Unlike most other birds, it cannot fly. Its wings have become flippers, which it uses to move through water. Its feet are webbed to help it swim. It feeds on fish and has a sharp beak for grabbing its slippery prey. All these special things help the penguin lead its particular way of life.

Temperate Woodland

Fox

Rabbits

Beetle

A Hot African Desert

Fennec fox

Jerboa

The variety of animal life

There are about a million different kinds, or species, of animals alive today. Hundreds of new species are discovered each year. Most are small animals, such as insects. But in 1987, a new species of lemur (a relative of the monkey) was discovered in Madagascar. It has been called the golden bamboo lemur. The sun-tailed guenon (a monkey) was found in central Africa a year later.

We may never know about all the animals that have lived on Earth. As we humans destroy tropical forests, we also kill species that have not been discovered.

Animals are different from other living things, such as plants. But all living things rely on each other in some way. No animal can survive on its own. It must feed on plants or other animals. Animals also depend on nonliving things such as water, oxygen, and sunlight. All living things are dependent in some way on other living and nonliving things.

Facts & Feats

- The giant squid is the largest water invertebrate. It can grow to 60 ft (18 m) long.

- The fastest-moving animal, the peregrine falcon, can dive at 224 miles (360 km) an hour.

- The largest and heaviest animal is the blue whale. It can grow to 100 ft (30 m) long and weigh over 200 tons.

- A flock of whooper swans were seen flying at a height of over 27,000 ft (8,100 m). This is almost as high as Mt. Everest, the world's highest mountain.

- The longest-lived animal is the ocean quahog, a thick-shelled clam. One is known to have lived 220 years.

- Arctic terns migrate from the Arctic, where they breed, to the Antarctic. Every year, they make a 25,000-mile (40,000-km) round trip.

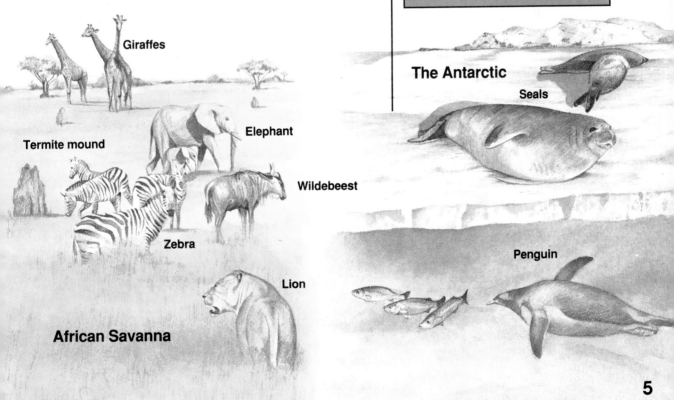

Giraffes

Termite mound

Elephant

Wildebeest

Zebra

Lion

African Savanna

The Antarctic

Seals

Penguin

Animal Groups

1 The lion shares certain features with other big cats. Most big cats roar, and all of them have hair extending to the front edge of their noses. Big cats are put together in the same group called a genus. We call the big cats' genus *Panthera*, so the scientific names of the big cats all start with *Panthera*.

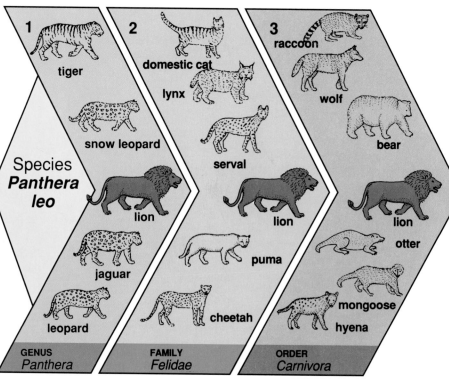

1
tiger
snow leopard
Species
Panthera leo
lion
jaguar
leopard
GENUS
Panthera

2
domestic cat
lynx
serval
lion
puma
cheetah
FAMILY
Felidae

3
raccoon
wolf
bear
lion
otter
mongoose
hyena
ORDER
Carnivora

▲

To understand animal groups, let's look at how biologists classify and name one animal, the lion. It is quite easy to tell a lion from other animals. It has certain features that no other animal has. So we call the lion a species. All individual lions belong to the same species. Biologists have given the lion a special scientific name, *Panthera leo*. No other species has this double name.

2 The big cats share some features with the small cats. So they are grouped together into the next group, which is called a family. The cat family includes all the different breeds of cat. The breeds include the domestic cat, the serval, lynx, cheetah, and lion. Scientists have given the name *Felidae* to the cat family.

3 All the meat-eating families, such as the cat, dog, bear, hyena, weasel, and raccoon families, have similar kinds of teeth. So they are put together into the next group, called an order. Biologists call the order of meat-eating animals *Carnivora*. We use a similar term, carnivore, for all meat-eating animals.

4 The next group is called a class. Each class includes several different orders. Each kind of animal in the lion's class has hair and feeds its young on mother's milk. Most give birth to live young. We call all animals in this class *Mammalia*. Human beings are placed in this group.

6

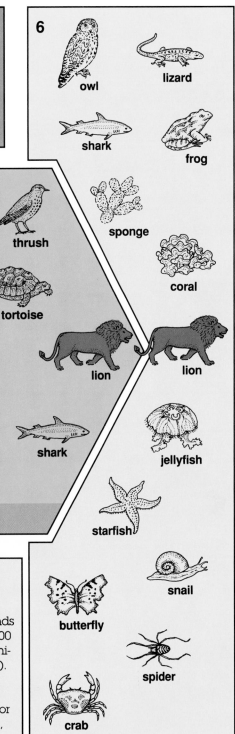

owl

lizard

shark

frog

sponge

coral

jellyfish

starfish

snail

butterfly

spider

crab

worm

ANIMAL KINGDOM

4

monkey

elephant

zebra

giraffe

kangaroo

lion

dolphin

aardvark

rat

walrus

platypus

CLASS
Mammalia

5

dolphin

owl

thrush

tortoise

newt

goldfish

lion

frog

lizard

shark

PHYLUM
Chordata (vertebrates)

5 The next group is called a phylum. The lion's phylum, called *Chordata*, includes all vertebrates (animals with a backbone) and another group called the protochordates. We have shown only vertebrates — animals with a backbone — as they are the most familiar to us. They include fish, amphibians, reptiles, birds, and mammals.

6 The last group is the animal kingdom. Here all animals are grouped together: about 42,000 kinds of vertebrates and 950,000 kinds of invertebrates (animals without backbones). A kingdom is the largest group. There are, of course, other kingdoms for plants, protozoans, fungi, and bacteria and blue-green algae.

Animal Evolution

Most of today's animals are different from their ancestors that lived millions of years ago. We know that species change over many generations. As they change, some become new species. Species that cannot adapt may die out and become extinct.

The dinosaurs

Perhaps the best-known animals that lived millions of years ago are dinosaurs. They ruled Earth for 140 million years. Some, such as Diplodocus, were as big as three semitrailer trucks, while others were no bigger than a crow. About 65 million years ago, they all died out. No one knows why. Some scientists think that the environment changed too quickly for them to adapt. We will never see a living dinosaur, because they are now all extinct.

Tyrannosaurus rex (90 million years ago)

Pteranodon — flying reptile (90 million years ago)

Diplodocus (140 million years ago)

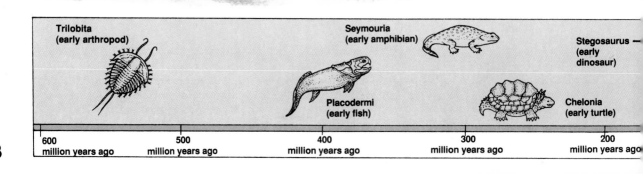

Trilobita (early arthropod)

Seymouria (early amphibian)

Stegosaurus — (early dinosaur)

Placodermi (early fish)

Chelonia (early turtle)

| 600 million years ago | 500 million years ago | 400 million years ago | 300 million years ago | 200 million years ago |

The record in the rocks

Most of what we know about dinosaurs and
other extinct animals comes from studying
their fossilized remains. Fossils are made when
bones, teeth, and shells of dead animals become rock while buried for millions of years.
Scientists dig up fossils and carefully piece
together the parts.

When life first appeared about 3.5 billion
years ago, it was in the form of simple single-
celled plants. The first soft-bodied animals
with cells but no backbone appeared about a
billion years ago. As time went by, new, more
complicated animals began to appear. The
first animals with backbones were primitive
fish that lived 500 million years ago. Some
animals moved from the sea onto land. Some
animals became more complex, while others
stayed simple or changed only a little. Other
animals became extinct. When animals
gradually change over millions of years, we
say they are evolving.

Living fossils ▲

A few animals have stayed
unchanged over millions of
years. We call these "living
fossils." Scientists had thought
that a primitive fish, the coelacanth, had been extinct for 70
million years, but in 1938 a
living coelacanth was caught
off of Africa. It stayed the same
all that time, probably because
its deep-sea home had not
changed much.

◀ **Time line:** This time line
shows when certain forms of
life first appeared on Earth. It
features such forms of animal life
as the first amphibians, the first
mammals, and the first ancestors
of human beings.

Pantothere
(early mammal)

Homo habilis
(early human)

Perissodactyla
(early horse)

Archaeopteryx
(early bird)

Glyptodon
(early armadillo)

| 200 | 100 | Recent |
| lion years ago | million years ago | Times |

Breathing

Caterpillar

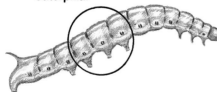

Spiracles

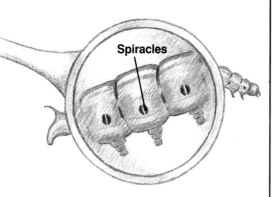

▲On the sides of an insect's body is a series of holes through which the insect breathes. The holes are connected to tubes in the insect's body. Air passes along these into the body.

Did You Know?

A fish from Africa called the lungfish can breathe in water and in the air. When the lakes where they live dry up, lungfish burrow into the mud and wrap themselves in a cocoon of slime. They can live like this for years, until the next rains come.

The dolphin. Like humans, the dolphin is a mammal. It breathes through lungs and has to hold its breath when it is underwater.

All animals need to breathe in oxygen in order to live. Land animals get oxygen from the air. Animals that live in the rivers and seas get oxygen from the water. They breathe out carbon dioxide.

Gases, such as oxygen and carbon dioxide, easily pass in and out of very small animals. When gases do this it is called diffusion. A single-celled animal breathes by diffusion. An earthworm can breathe like this through its skin. Its skin must always be moist for diffusion to take place. But larger animals need a special breathing system.

Breathing in air

On the sides of an insect's body, there are holes called spiracles. Air passes through the spiracles and deep into the insect's body through a network of tubes.

Breathing in water

Animals that breathe underwater use gills. A fish takes water into its mouth and passes it

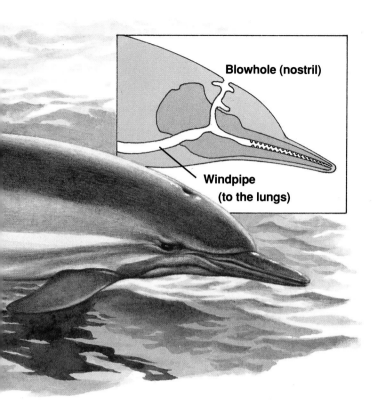

Blowhole (nostril)

Windpipe
(to the lungs)

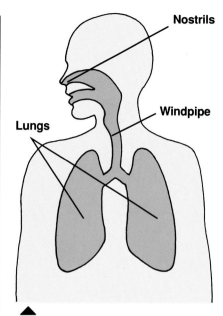

Nostrils

Windpipe

Lungs

People breathe by using lungs to move air in and out of the body through nostrils. Dolphins have a nostril on top of the head called a "blowhole." They also breathe using lungs. Unlike fish, dolphins cannot stay underwater very long.

A fish breathes by taking water in through its mouth. It gets oxygen by passing the water over its gills. Blood vessels in the gills take out the oxygen and carry it through the fish's body. Waste water is pushed out of the gill flaps. So is carbon dioxide.

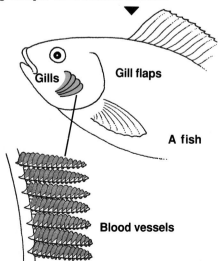

Gills

Gill flaps

A fish

Blood vessels

over its gills. A fish's gills are made of many thin, fleshy strands. Gills, like lungs, have a large surface to get as much oxygen as possible. The gills of young lungfish are easily seen. The gills of the lobster lie near the base of its legs.

Not all animals living in water use gills to breathe. Some, such as the water scorpion, are air-breathers. This insect has a long tube on the end of its body. It uses this like a snorkel, coming to the surface and poking it out of the water.

Whales and dolphins are air-breathing mammals, even though they live in water. Their nostrils are at the top of the head — the blowhole. When a whale comes to the surface it "blows," or breathes out, through its blowhole. The spray that appears is its breath. Whales and dolphins can hold their breath for a long time under water. A male sperm whale can stay underwater for nearly two hours when diving very deep. People can stay under water for only a minute or two.

Hot and Cold Animals

Warm blood, cold blood

Human beings, like other mammals and all birds, are warm-blooded. They all have a warm body temperature that doesn't change much. Their bodies get energy from food and oxygen, and this energy creates heat to keep them warm.

All animals lose heat from their bodies. People use clothes to keep warm, so when it gets cold, they put on more layers. Mammals have fur and birds have feathers to help them keep in their body heat.

Small mammals and birds lose that heat more quickly than large animals. Shrews, for instance, must eat constantly to make energy to keep warm. If a shrew goes without food for more than a few hours, it will die.

All invertebrates, as well as amphibians, fish, and reptiles, are cold-blooded. These animals have a body temperature that changes. In cold weather, a lizard's body temperature is low. In hot weather, it has a

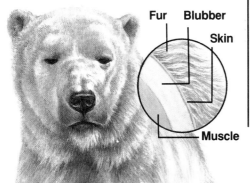

Fur Blubber
Skin
Muscle

Some Warm-blooded Animals

Polar bear

Shrew

Dolphin

Penguin

Deer

Bat

Tarsier

Pigeon

12

high body temperature. Cold-blooded animals cannot keep their body temperatures the same all the time the way warm-blooded animals do.

Getting away from it all

Finding enough food in winter is difficult for some mammals and birds. The dormouse builds up extra fat layers during summer. In winter its heartbeat and breathing slow down, its temperature drops, and it goes into hibernation, a kind of deep sleep. Hibernating animals use less energy. Their fat gives them enough energy to live through winter without eating.

Some birds, such as swallows, avoid cold weather by migrating. They fly thousands of miles to warmer countries where they can find enough food.

All cold-blooded animals have to get away from the cold of winter. Otherwise, they would die. Lizards, snakes, and frogs hibernate in holes underground. Some butterflies spend the winter in sheltered corners of sheds or garages.

Warm-blooded animals:
- Have fur or feathers to keep them warm
- Have a body temperature that stays the same most of the time
- Rely on food to make their body heat

Cold-blooded animals:
- Rely on heat from the Sun to keep up their body heat
- Most cold-blooded animals have to hibernate during a freezing winter

Some Cold-blooded Animals

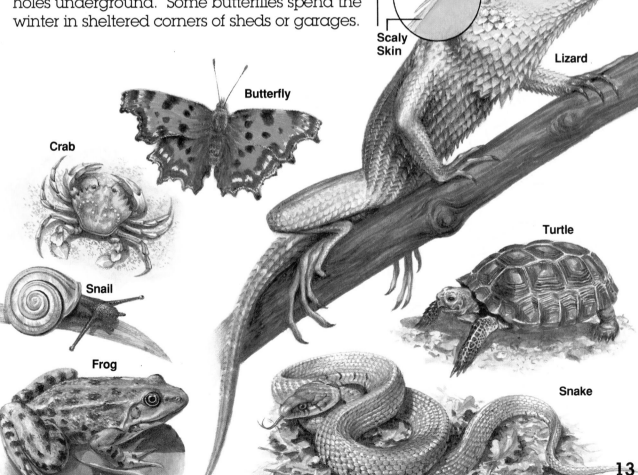

Muscle

Scaly Skin

Lizard

Butterfly

Crab

Snail

Frog

Turtle

Snake

13

2: | MOVEMENT

Moving on Land

Animals that move on land must have some kind of support. They get that support from their limbs and skeleton. Human beings are supported by two limbs — their legs. Cats, dogs, and many other animals are supported on four legs. Some animals have more than four legs. Insects have six; spiders have eight; crabs and their relatives have ten; centipedes and millipedes have many more. Snakes and some lizards have no legs at all. They move by twisting their bodies into an "S" shape and pressing them against the ground.

The bones of the skeleton keep animals upright. Muscles, attached to bones, enable animals to move. Muscles use energy to move the bones, which in turn move different parts of their bodies.

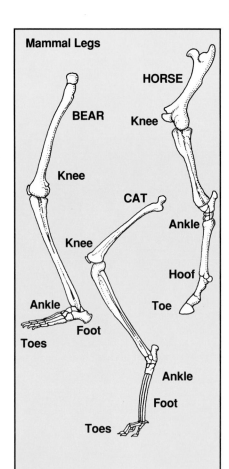

Mammal Legs

BEAR

HORSE

Knee

Knee

CAT

Ankle

Knee

Hoof

Ankle

Toe

Foot

Toes

Ankle

Foot

Toes

The legs of these animals are built differently, so each animal moves at different speeds. The bear puts all of its foot flat on the ground. The cat puts only part of its foot on the ground, and the horse stands on its toe, which we call its hoof. The smaller the area of foot touching the ground, the faster the animal can go.

A SPRINTING CHEETAH — THE FASTEST LAND ANIMAL

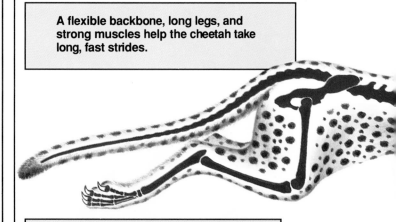

A flexible backbone, long legs, and strong muscles help the cheetah take long, fast strides.

Unlike other cats, the cheetah keeps its claws out for gripping like spikes on athletic shoes.

Supporting skeletons

Vertebrates have an internal skeleton that is made of bone and is inside the body. Invertebrates have an external skeleton — their shell or carapace. Both vertebrates and invertebrates use muscles to move.

Fast runners

The cheetah is the fastest land animal. It can run at 70 miles (112 km) an hour. It has a thin, lithe body, long legs, and claws that grip like spikes in running shoes. Its long tail helps it balance when it swerves. All these adaptations help it run fast. But the cheetah is a sprinter that can only run at top speed over a short distance.

To run fast, animals need long legs. Only small areas of their feet can be touching the ground at any moment as they run.

Humans and bears are flat-footed compared with other animals and move more slowly because their feet touch the ground almost completely. Only part of a dog's foot touches the ground. It stands on tiptoe. The only part of a horse's foot touching the ground is its toenail, or hoof.

▲ Crabs are invertebrates. A crab's skeleton is on the outside of its body. It moves sideways across the sand using its eight legs. Two other legs are pincers.

Facts & Feats

• A female red kangaroo covered a distance of almost 43 ft (13 m) in one bound.

• The farthest-jumping frog is the South African sharp-nosed frog. One leaped 9 ft 10 inches (3 m).

• Snakes do not have legs, but boas and pythons have two tiny remnants of hind legs. These do not help them move but are used in mating to grasp a partner.

• The black mamba is the fastest-moving snake. It can move at about 20 miles (32 km) an hour.

• The fastest land animal is the cheetah, known to run up to 70 miles (112 km) an hour.

• An ostrich has only two toes on each foot. It can run up to 40 miles (64 km) an hour.

• The common garden snail has a top speed of 52.8 yards (47.5 m) an hour. This means it would take a snail more than 33 hours to travel one mile (about 2/3 km). The cheetah can run this far in just over 50 seconds!

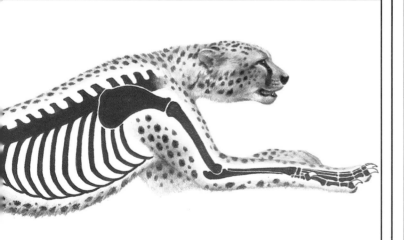

Hard footpads have ridges that act like tire treads to give extra grip.

Moving in Trees

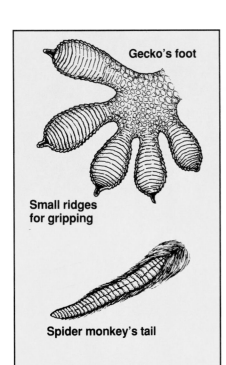

Gecko's foot

Small ridges for gripping

Spider monkey's tail

Did You Know?

Tree frogs and some lizards (like geckos or anolis lizards) have toes with swollen ends. They can hold on to glass upside-down! The toes look as if they stick like the suction cup of a toy arrow. In fact, the toes have tiny ridges and hooks. These tightly grip tiny cracks in surfaces we cannot easily see.

Moving in trees can be dangerous for any animal. A fall can mean injury or death. Animals moving in trees need good grips and good eyesight to judge distances. They may also need special means of keeping their balance if they are to move quickly through the trees.

The graspers

Human hands are grasping hands. Each hand has an opposable thumb, or a thumb that faces our fingers. Our nearest relatives, monkeys and apes, have similar hands. Hands like ours help monkeys and apes grip the tree branches.

Some monkeys from Central and South America have prehensile tails, or tails that grip. Other tree-living animals also have prehensile tails. Birds that perch in trees have feet designed for grasping. They generally have three toes in the front and one toe in the back of each foot.

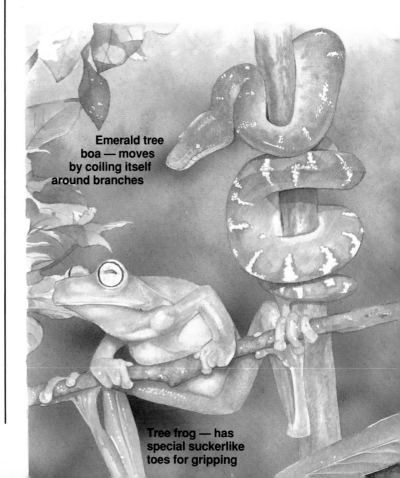

Emerald tree boa — moves by coiling itself around branches

Tree frog — has special suckerlike toes for gripping

These birds grip tree branches when resting. Woodpeckers have two toes in the front and two toes in the back of each foot, so their feet can grip onto the side of a tree. Woodpeckers can thus move up or down the trunk of a tree as they look for food.

The swingers

Gibbons from southeast Asia swing through the trees. They use their hands like hooks to hang on branches and move by swinging from branch to branch. This way of moving is called brachiation.

Leapers and balancers

Some mammals are very fast-moving tree dwellers. Squirrels dash along tree branches. Their sharp claws grip the branch tightly as they run along. Their powerful back legs allow them to jump from tree to tree. A squirrel's tail helps it balance as it sways on the thinner branches.

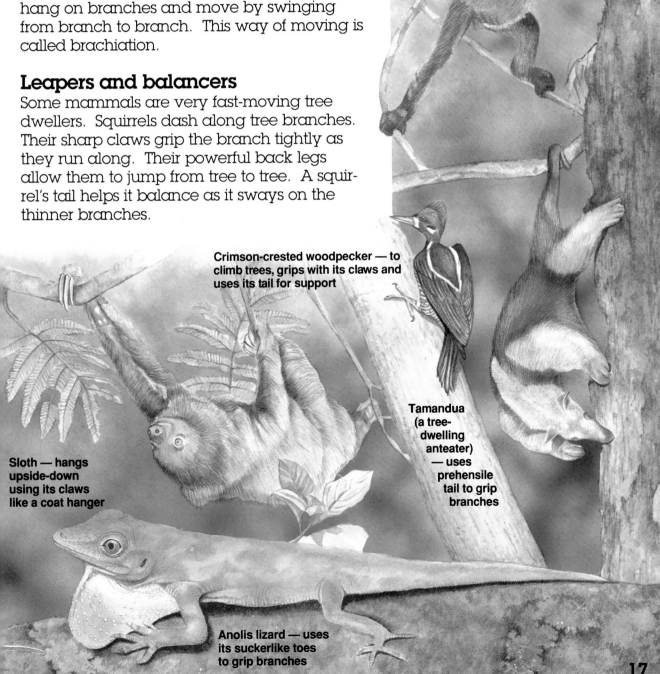

Spider monkey — grips branches with extra limb, its prehensile tail

Crimson-crested woodpecker — to climb trees, grips with its claws and uses its tail for support

Tamandua (a tree-dwelling anteater) — uses prehensile tail to grip branches

Sloth — hangs upside-down using its claws like a coat hanger

Anolis lizard — uses its suckerlike toes to grip branches

17

Moving in Earth

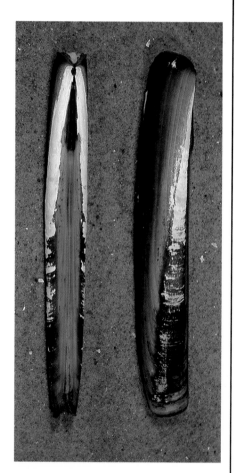

▲ The jackknife clam uses its long, muscular foot to burrow deep into the sand.

The armadillo from South America has powerful front legs with strong claws. These are used for digging into the ground. ▶

Many animals make their homes underground. This helps them hide from their enemies, keep warm when it is cold outside, and keep cool when it is too hot.

Tools for digging

Most burrowing animals are adapted for digging. The aardvark, a termite-eating mammal from Africa, has strong front legs and wide, thick claws. It uses its legs and claws to dig its burrows. Armadillos from South America and wombats from Australia also dig burrows with their powerful claws.

The mole is specially adapted for moving underground. Its front feet are flat and broad, with stout claws. They work like a pair of shovels. Its fur is short and velvety. The fur moves easily backward or forward and never gets clogged with earth.

The mole is almost blind, but its sensitive whiskers and strong sense of smell are more useful underground than eyesight. Its powerful feet and claws dig through soil.

An earthworm eats its way through soil, taking soil in one end and passing it out of the other.

The earthworm grips the side of its tunnel with bristly hairs. Its muscles move it through the tunnel.

Moles have tiny eyes. Good eyesight is not needed underground, but a good sense of smell and touch is important. The mole's whiskers tell it what's happening at the front. Its sensitive tail tells it what is going on in back. This is important, since moles cannot easily turn around in their tunnels.

Burrowers without backbones

Earthworms, moles' favorite food, burrow by pushing aside loose soil with their muscular bodies. They burrow through very hard soil by eating their way through it.

A worm's body is divided into segments. Each segment has four pairs of bristles that help the worm grip the soil. While one part of the worm is anchored to the ground, it stretches out another part.

The jackknife clam is a mollusk that lives on the seashore. It burrows into mud and sand using its long, muscular foot. Pushing its foot deep into the sand, it burrows more quickly than people can dig. It can sense vibrations and will burrow away from danger.

▲ Animals that live underground adapt to their special environment. The mole and the earthworm look different from each other. But they are both expert underground movers.

▲ The sandfish is not really a fish at all. It is a lizard with a very streamlined body that helps it move (or "swim") through the sand. Notice its tiny legs.

Moving in Air

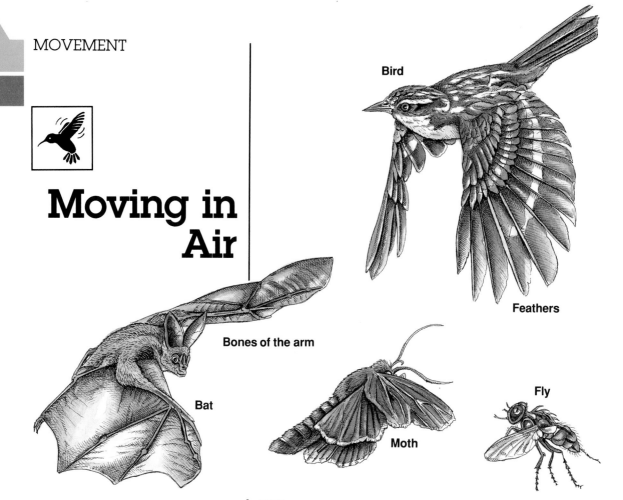

Bird

Feathers

Bones of the arm

Bat

Moth

Fly

▲ Birds, bats, and insects all have wings that enable them to fly. The bat is a flying mammal — the only mammal that can control its flight. Its wings are made of a sheet of skin stretched over its bones. Birds are the only animals with feathers. Powerful muscles attached to each wing help them beat their wings and fly.

Did You Know?

Beetles can fly. Like other insects, they have two pairs of wings, but one pair is quite hard and forms the beetle's outer shell. These wings protect the second pair that lies underneath.

Wings

Animals that move in the air can fly, glide, or do both. All flying animals have wings. They include insects, birds, and bats.

Wings have a wide, flat shape to help push an animal through the air. Insects generally have two pairs of wings that are very delicate but are made stronger by a network of veins. Sometimes the front and back wings hook together to make an insect look as if it has only one pair of wings.

Birds' wings are made of feathers arranged together to make a light but strong wing. Birds' feathers are attached to the flesh on the bone in the wing. Because birds' larger bones are hollow with a honeycombed structure inside, they are light but strong. Bats have a thin membrane of skin for their wings. Their arm and finger bones support this membrane, which stretches to their back legs.

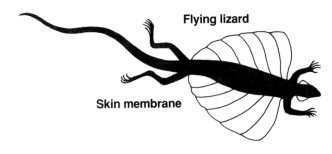

Flying lizard

Skin membrane

Gliders

Other animal species are gliders. The flying fish has big pectoral fins that look like wings but do not flap like bird wings. Flying fish leap out of the water to escape their enemies. They can glide above the surface of the water for up to 3,600 ft (1,100 m).

The flying squirrel lives in trees. Like the bat, this gliding mammal has a thin membrane that stretches between its arms and legs. It escapes danger or moves about the forest by gliding from tree to tree.

The flying frog uses its membranes in the same way. Its webbed feet act like gliding wings, catching the wind to keep it aloft.

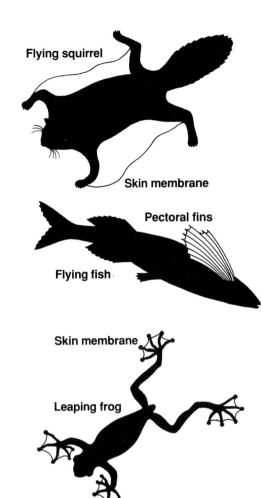

Flying squirrel

Skin membrane

Pectoral fins

Flying fish

Skin membrane

Leaping frog

▲ Gliding animals, unlike bats, birds, or insects, cannot control their flight. But they are able to glide through the air from a high point to a lower point.

◀ Birds' curved wings help them fly, and their strong muscles provide the power to move through the air. The bones are hollow but strong, so they are very light.

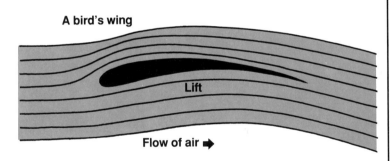

A bird's wing

Lift

Flow of air ➡

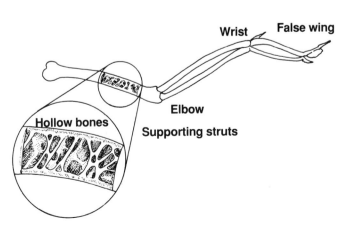

Wrist   **False wing**

Hollow bones

Elbow

Supporting struts

Parachuting spiders

Some tiny spiders float in the air like parachutes. By releasing a long silk thread that catches the wind, they drift thousands of feet up in the air and travel for miles.

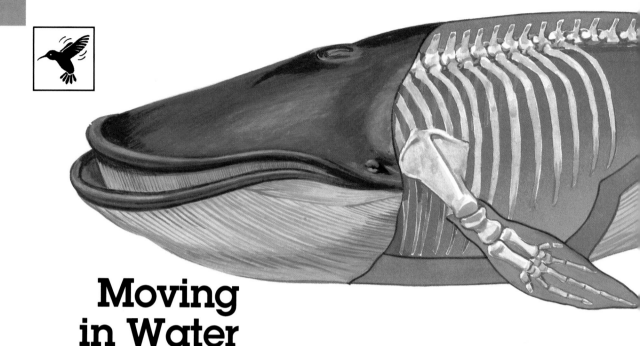

Moving in Water

The seal, the penguin, and ▲ the pike are creatures that live in water all or some of the time. The pike uses its tail and fins to move around; the penguin and seal use flippers. They all have a stream-lined shape for moving in water.

Water is 800 times more dense than air. This means it is harder to move in, but it also means it can support animals' bodies. You can float in water but not in air!

The blue whale is the biggest animal ever to have lived. It can grow to 90 ft (27 m) and weigh 150 tons. On land it would be too heavy to move.

Streamlining

As an aquatic mammal, the blue whale breathes air like humans, even though it spends all its life in the sea. Aquatic animals have special adaptations to help them move in water. A whale is streamlined — narrow at both ends and thicker in the middle. This is the best shape for moving through water. It moves by beating its broad, flat tail up and down.

Millions of years ago, the ancestors of the whale lived on land. They had legs and were much smaller. When they moved to living in water their legs lost their use. All that is left of

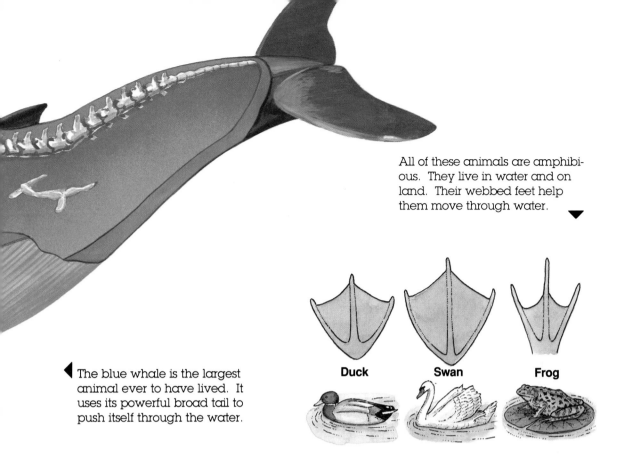

All of these animals are amphibious. They live in water and on land. Their webbed feet help them move through water. ▼

Duck   **Swan**   **Frog**

◀ The blue whale is the largest animal ever to have lived. It uses its powerful broad tail to push itself through the water.

the legs are several small bones in the whale's flippers. The picture above shows these bones, as well as the pelvic bone, which was once attached to the back legs of the whale's ancestors.

Swimming styles

Most fish push themselves forward with their tails. The coral fish rows with large pectoral fins. The sea snake bends and twists its body, its flat tail helping to move it along. The water boatman is an insect that swims on its back. Its long, thin legs, with hairs on the third pair, help it swim. The cuttlefish moves very fast by using a kind of jet propulsion. It sucks water into a tube in its body and squirts the water out quickly to push it along.

Animals that live on land and in the water are amphibious. Many of them have webbed feet. You can see from the illustration above how the skin stretches between the bones of an amphibian's toes. Like the flat tail of a fish, this skin helps the animal push itself through the water.

Facts & Feats

▪ The fastest-moving fish, the sailfish, can move at 68 miles (110 km) per hour.

▪ The grebe is a water bird. Its feet, unlike a duck's, are positioned at the end of its body, which makes it difficult for it to balance and walk on land.

▪ The fastest-swimming mammal is the killer whale. One was timed at 34.5 miles (55.5 km) per hour.

▪ The gray whale makes a huge annual migration of almost 12,000 miles (20,000 km) from the Bering Sea to California and Mexico and back.

▪ The flying fish has been known to reach a height of 36 ft (11 m) above water, travel a distance of 3,000 ft (1,000 m) out of water, and "fly" at 35 mph (56 kph).

3: EATING AND BEING EATEN

Hunters and Killers

Predatory animals kill and eat other animals — their prey. Most predators must hunt, chase, catch, and kill their prey. Each species has its own way of hunting and its own set of weapons for killing.

A tiger kills
The Bengal tiger eats antelope and deer. Once the tiger has seen its prey, it stalks it carefully and slowly. The tiger keeps its sharp claws hidden in sheaths within its paws.

Super swallowers

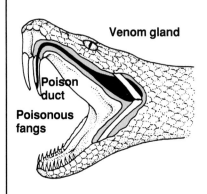

Venom gland

Poison duct

Poisonous fangs

The rattlesnake catches its prey using a poisonous liquid called venom. The snake injects venom into its victim through hollow fangs at the front of its mouth. Venom can kill a rat or mouse in a matter of minutes. By loosening and stretching some bones in its jaw, the snake slowly swallows its victim in one piece. Strong digestive juices break down everything, including bones and fur.

Soft pads on its feet help it creep up on the antelope quietly. Its striped coat gives excellent camouflage in the long grass. When it is close enough, the tiger rushes its prey. Seizing the prey by the throat, it sinks in its long canine teeth.

The tiger unsheathes its sharp claws to grip the struggling animal. Once it is dead, the tiger tears off large pieces of meat, using its carnassial (cutting) teeth.

Seashore soup

The starfish eats mussels, clams, and other mollusks. It wraps its body around the mussel, gripping tightly with its feet. It pulls the mussel's shells apart and pushes its stomach out of its own body and between the mussel's shells. Its digestive juices pour onto the soft parts of the mussel. The starfish then absorbs the mussel "soup" through its stomach.

▲ This bird is a golden eagle. Its hooked beak is used to rip and tear the flesh off its prey.

◀ The Bengal tiger is an expert hunter. It will quietly stalk its prey until it is close enough to leap and kill it.

Drilling for "soup"

The dog whelk turns limpets into "soup." Using a kind of drill that is part of its body, it makes a hole through a limpet's shell, pours digestive juices into the limpet, and sucks up the resulting "soup" through the holes.

Ambushers, Anglers, and Trappers

The chameleon can change ▲ color when it wants to. It usually does this to camouflage itself.

Not all animals chase after their prey. Some wait patiently for their next live meal to come to them. They may use specially adapted parts of their body to catch their prey. Others may set traps.

Ambushers

Some animals stay quietly watching and waiting for their victim to come within range. Frogs, crocodiles, and some spiders are ambushers, as is the chameleon, a lizard that lives in Africa and Madagascar. It camouflages itself by changing color to fit in with its background. It keeps very still and is hard to see. One eye looks forward while the other watches what is going on behind. It catches insects with a sticky tongue that is longer than its own body! It can shoot its tongue out of its mouth quickly to catch insects.

Sea anemones are animals that look like plants. Their thick stalk holds them onto rocks and the seabed. They look beautiful, but their "flower" is a ring of deadly tentacles that grab fish, stick tiny poisonous darts into the fish, and then push the fish into the anemone's mouth.

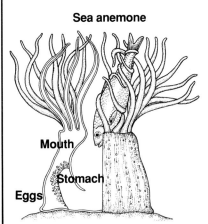

Sea anemone

Mouth

Stomach

Eggs

This sea anemone has stunned a fish with its poisonous ▲ tentacles. It will push the fish into its stomach to be digested and eventually spit the waste material back out.

Anglers

The alligator snapping turtle and the anglerfish both "fish" for their food by laying bait to catch their prey. The snapping turtle's tongue looks like a worm. It opens its mouth and wiggles its tongue to attract fish. When the fish come close enough, it grabs them. The anglerfish uses a long spine like a fishing rod on its head (above).

Trappers

Some animals, like the ant lion (right), build traps to catch their prey. This creature lies at the bottom of a little funnel-shaped pit of sand waiting for an insect, like an ant, to fall into the pit. Some spider species trap insects by building webs made of silk and covered with glue. The spider stays on the edge of the web holding onto a single thread. When an insect enters the web, it becomes trapped. As it struggles to get away, it sends out vibrations. The spider rushes out and bites the insect with poisonous fangs. It may wrap up its meal in thread and store it away to eat later.

The anglerfish lies in the dark ▲ depths of the sea, dangling a piece of bait from its head to attract small fish. When the fish come close enough, it opens its mouth and eats them.

At the bottom of a sandy ▲ funnel lies the ant lion larva. This picture shows its jaws wide open, ready, like an animal trap, to close on a small insect that has fallen into its pit.

Plant Eaters

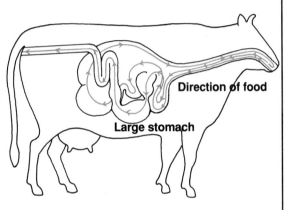

▲ The cow swallows grass, which passes down into the first part of its stomach. Having finished eating, the cow rests. Small amounts of partially digested grass are brought up to be chewed for a second time. This well-chewed mouthful moves into another chamber of the stomach. Here, microscopic creatures help digest the grass even more.

Direction of food

Large stomach

Did You Know?

The fruits of most plants are always popular food for animals. The coconut crab takes a lot of trouble to find its favorite fruit. It cannot crack coconuts open, but it looks everywhere it can for broken coconuts to eat.

Animals that eat only plants are called herbivores. Plants grow just about everywhere, so they are an easy food to find. Herbivores eat plant leaves, seeds, fruit, roots, sap, and even tree bark.

Hungry herbivores

Giraffes enjoy eating the leaves of the thorny acacia tree. Their long tongues and floppy lips twist around the twigs to strip the leaves away. Parrots use their powerful beaks to crack open the hard shells of nuts and seeds. A butterfly looks for nectar by searching the petals of a flower with its proboscis — a long, hollow tongue that is used like a straw to suck up the sugary nectar from inside the flower.

Grass, leaves, and bark are not very nutritious foods. They are also difficult to digest, but some mammals have found a way to make the most of plant food. Once a cow has taken its first mouthful, it keeps chewing. This breaks the grass down until it is ready for swallowing into the stomach. A cow keeps eating until it has filled its large stomach. Most cattle, sheep, giraffes, antelope, and deer have big, bulging stomachs to hold all that vegetation. When full, they move to a quiet, safe place where they chew the cud, or ruminate. Ruminating mammals bring up their

These are animals from the African savanna. Colobus monkeys eat leaves from trees. Tall giraffes stretch up to browse on the leaves. Antelope both browse and graze on the grass. Zebras eat only the grass. Birds eat seeds, fruit, and nuts.

Mouths that adapt!

The black rhinoceros and the white rhinoceros have different kinds of mouths. Black rhinos have pointed upper lips for grasping and browse on leaves. White rhinos have wide, flat upper lips for clipping grass.

▼

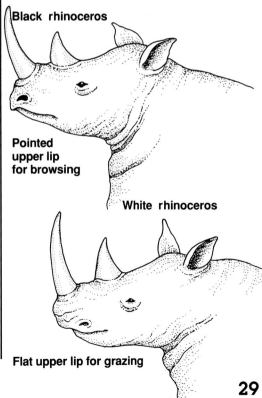

Black rhinoceros

Pointed upper lip for browsing

White rhinoceros

Flat upper lip for grazing

food and chew it for a second time. Tiny microscopic creatures in the animal's stomach help break down the plant material. With this extra help and by ruminating, these plant-eaters get more nutrition from their food.

Grazers and browsers

On African savannas many herbivores live together: antelope, elephants, giraffes, rhinos, hippopotamuses, and zebras. Some graze on grass; others browse on leaves; some do both. Since these animals do not all eat exactly the same plants, they do not compete with each other for the same food.

913268

Omnivores and Scavengers

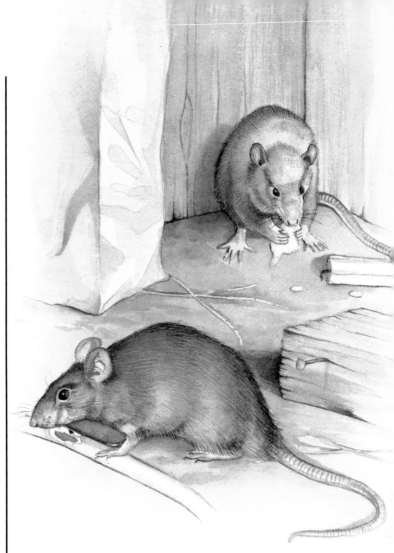

Rats can live almost anywhere. ▶ If nothing better is around, they will eat candle wax and the plastic insulation around wires. The fact that they are not too fussy about what they eat helps them survive in many different environments.

A dung beetle rolling away a ball of dung. This will provide both the beetle and its young with food. ▼

Animals that eat both plants and other animals are called omnivores. This means that they can eat almost anything.

Adaptable omnivores

Human beings and the brown rat are both omnivores. The brown rat has a wide taste in food. It will eat candle wax, soap, even the plastic insulation around electric cables.

Choosing a wide variety of food can help an animal survive. In the wild, the European red fox eats meat, insects, worms, and fruit. Because it is not too choosy about what it eats, it can also live in towns. Foxes in cities are more omnivorous than their country cousins. They raid city trash cans, eating food scraps thrown out by humans.

Other omnivores include bears, pigs, blackbirds, and wasps. Chimpanzees eat mainly plants and fruit, but they also eat termites. They will even kill and eat baby antelope and baboons.

Scavengers

Many omnivorous animals are scavengers. They eat rotting waste, such as dead plants and animals. They may even eat the dung of other animals. These animals keep the natural world tidy and recycle the world's supply of natural materials.

When a fly eats rotting food, the fly becomes food for something else. Eventually all this waste material gets recycled. Dung beetles roll dung into balls and bury them so they have a supply of dung ready for eating. Vultures and jackals feed mainly on the bodies of dead animals. Wood lice often feed on rotting vegetation.

▲ Vultures do not kill animals for food. They look for the carcasses of dead animals to feed on.

Chimpanzees catch termites by dipping a twig into the termite nest. The insects attack the twig and hold on tight with their jaws. The chimpanzee simply pulls out the twig and eats the termites attached to it.
▼

Specialist Feeders

Blood meals

Vampire bats, leeches, and mosquitoes are some of the animals that feed on blood, a rich, nutritious food. All animals that feed on the blood of others are specially adapted to do so, and the bite of these attackers is so sharp that many victims do not feel it. Vampire bats have razor-sharp teeth. A mosquito has some sharp stabbing mouth parts as well as a tube for sucking blood.

Blood quickly clots to stop wounds from bleeding. All blood-feeding animals have a chemical in their saliva that stops blood from clotting, so they can drink without the blood drying up. No blood feeder directly kills its victim, but it can carry and spread dangerous diseases. Vampire bats carry rabies and mosquitoes carry malaria.

Vampire bat

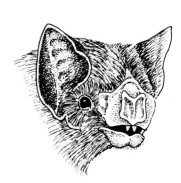

Sharp upper teeth (incisors)

A vampire bat has sharp teeth ▶ used to make a wound in its victim and channels in its tongue to help blood flow into its mouth. These bats have been known to drink so much blood that they become too heavy to fly away.

The female mosquito has a set of ▶ organs in the proboscis that can puncture the skin of animals to get at the blood. Some mosquitoes carry harmful diseases, such as malaria, which they can pass on to the animals they bite, including humans.

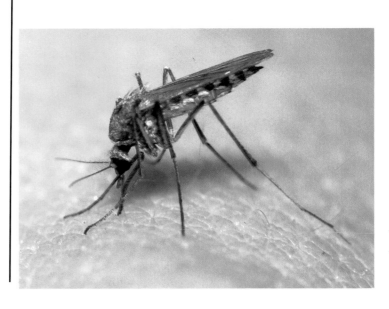

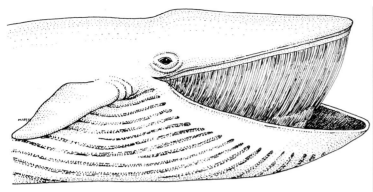

The whale's grooved throat works like an accordion and stretches out to take in lots of seawater.

 The baleen whale does not have any teeth. Instead, it has a horny material, called whalebone, in its mouth. This is attached to the upper jaw and can be up to 13 ft (4 m) in length. They use their whalebone to filter out tiny animals, such as krill, from the seawater.

Feeding by filtering

Millions of microscopic plants and animals, called plankton, live in water. Some animals have special ways of straining or filtering off these tasty items from the water. Because the plankton are so small, their predators need to take in great quantities of water in order to filter out a decent meal.

The fan worm lives in the sea. It has feathery tentacles, with tiny cells that trap bits of food with a sticky slime. These tentacles pass the food along to the worm's mouth like a conveyor belt.

The flamingo is a strange-looking bird. Its long legs and long neck are useful for walking in shallow water looking for food. It catches food by putting its beak into the water and moving it from side to side. On the inside of a flamingo's beak are filters that look like combs. It feeds by pumping water through its beak. The tiny organisms in the water get caught on the combs.

Blue whales and right whales are members of a group called baleen whales. Instead of teeth, they have whalebone, or baleen, in their mouths which forms a "curtain" to trap shrimp-like animals called krill. Each time a blue whale opens its mouth, it takes in many gallons of water and catches millions of krill.

Did You Know?

The rare giant panda's ancestors were probably meat-eaters. Today, giant pandas eat mainly bamboo plants. Since they come from thick bamboo forests in China, they probably became specialized bamboo feeders because bamboo grew all around them. They evolved an extra "thumb" to allow them to pick and hold the bamboo. But becoming so specialized can be risky. Much of the bamboo forest in China is dying, and pandas now have problems getting enough food.

How Not to Be Eaten

▲ Stick insects look like twigs on trees and bushes. To avoid being noticed by hungry predators, they move very slowly, and their camouflage protects them.

The ptarmigan changes its color with the seasons. Its summer plumage blends in with the vegetation. In winter it turns white, which helps it stay hidden against a background of snow. ▶

Many animals try to avoid being eaten by hiding from their predators. They have certain shapes or colors, called camouflage, that help them do this. Stick insects look like the twigs of trees where they live. One kind of caterpillar looks like a bird dropping on a leaf. The chameleon can change colors quickly to match different backgrounds.

Safe shells and sharp spines

When danger threatens, many animals escape by running away. But others move too slowly and need other forms of protection. Some may have shells or spines to protect them. Snails and turtles hide in their shells when they are attacked. The armadillo's hard skin protects it like a shell. Many other animals are protected by spines. The hedgehog, porcupine, and sea urchin are all prickly. The spines of the porcupine and sea urchin are loose. Any animal that gets too close risks a painful pricking.

A ptarmigan in summer plumage

Poisonous protection

Some animals use a poison, or venom, to protect themselves. The deadly stonefish of the Indo-Pacific Ocean, the stingray, and the weaver fish all have venomous spines through which venom enters the attacker's body. Attacking animals may become very ill or even die. These animals use their venomous spines and stings only in self-defense, not to catch prey.

Colorful warnings

Bees, wasps, coral snakes, and skunks all have striped patterns that make them easy to see. These colors and patterns, called warning colors, tell other animals that they might be dangerous. Bees and wasps sting. Coral snakes have a poisonous bite. The skunk does a handstand, presents its bottom, and sprays a lingering, irritating, and smelly fluid at its attacker. Predators quickly learn to leave these animals alone!

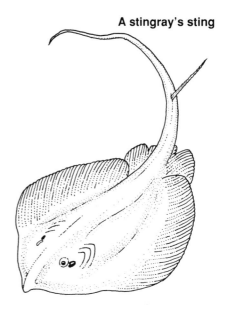

A stingray's sting

▲ The sting in a stingray's tail can be flicked out and ready to strike when it is needed to defend the ray from a predator.

A ptarmigan in winter plumage

Cunning confusion

Eye spots on a moth's wing turn it from a tasty morsel into a staring, threatening face. A lizard's tail drops off and wriggles, confusing a predator. The lizard escapes. A hog-nosed snake suddenly rolls over and pretends to be dead. All these actions confuse an attacker, giving the animal a chance to survive.

4: THE SENSES

Animal Eyes

Some animals, such as flatworms, have very simple eyes and can see only light and dark. They live in dark places under rocks and avoid the light. Insects have compound eyes made up of many tiny tubes, each like a complete eye. The more tubes in a compound eye, the better the insect's vision. A dragonfly has 10,000 of these tubes in each compound eye!

Human eyes have a different design. The human eye is like a camera with a pupil that opens and closes to control how much light enters the eye. A lens helps focus vision. The retina at the back of the eye picks up the image of what a person is looking at and passes it on into the brain.

All vertebrates have a "camera" eye like this. The only invertebrates with such a complicated eye design are the squid and octopus. We can see colors, and animals

▲ Insects have compound eyes made up of thousands of tiny tubes positioned on the side of their heads. This gives them a wide field of vision.

These photographs both show the eye of a bird. The first shows it as a human would see it. The second shows it as a bee would see it. The bee has a compound eye. This means its vision is different from ours. It sees thousands of separate images through the tubes that make up its eye. ▶

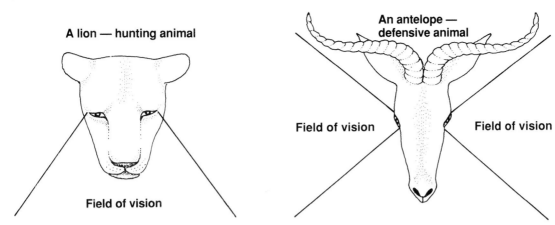

A lion — hunting animal

Field of vision

An antelope — defensive animal

Field of vision   Field of vision

that are brightly colored can also see colors. Otherwise, why be brightly colored? Many colorful birds, reptiles, and fish can see colors, while many mammals, such as dogs, antelope, and rodents, can only see a limited spectrum of colors, or even only in black and white.

Eyes for life

An animal's eyes tell us a lot about how it lives. A hunting animal like a lion or tiger has eyes at the front of its head to help it judge distance when it attacks its prey. A hunted animal like an antelope, deer, or rabbit has eyes at the sides of its head. It can eat and watch out for predators attacking from any angle at the same time, but it cannot judge distance as well.

▲ The lion, a hunting animal, has a narrow, focused field of vision, which helps it single out its prey. The antelope, its prey, has a wide field of vision. It can detect movement in a wide arc around its body which will alert it to danger.

A camera eye

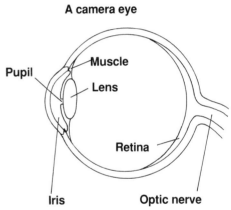

Pupil

Muscle

Lens

Retina

Iris   Optic nerve

▲ All vertebrate animals have an eye that works like a camera. The amount of light that enters the eye is controlled by the pupil. If there is a lot of light, the pupil will become narrower to let in less light. At night, the pupil opens wide to let in all available light.

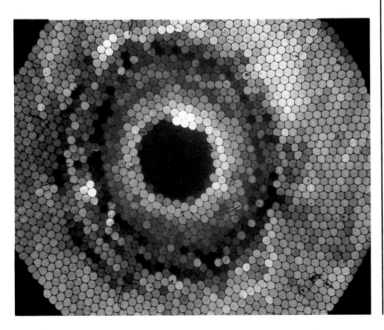

Smelling and Tasting

▲ A wolf's nose is long and very sensitive. At its tip is a bare piece of skin that is always moist. This helps it pick up smells.

A moth uses its large antennae to pick up smells in the air around it.

▶

Smells are chemicals that float around in the air or are dissolved in water or saliva. Animals have organs of smell and taste, called olfactory organs, that pick up these sensations. Noses and tongues are olfactory organs. Smells can be picked up from a long way, and taste is used up close.

A world of smells

Wolves live in a world of smells. The human sense of smell cannot compare with a wolf's. The moist, bare skin on its nose helps it pick up a wide range of smells. A wolf can follow trails of smells left by other animals. Sharks and piranhas smell blood dissolved in water. Their sense of smell is very sensitive. Sharks can smell an injured animal in the water 1/4 mile (0.4 km) away.

Salmon can remember smells. They are born in rivers and swim to the sea, where they spend most of their life. But they return to rivers to breed. Their sense of smell helps them find the river where they first hatched.

Smelly signals

Smells may be used by one animal to signal to another. A chemical called a pheromone is a

◀ This male lion appears to be making a funny face because it has smelled the scent of a female. Sexual activity is often started by special scents given off by the female animal to attract the attention of a male.

sex signal released by a female and picked up by a male of the species. This will tell him that she is ready to mate. When the female gypsy moth is ready to breed, she releases tiny amounts of pheromone into the air. Male gypsy moths have large antennae that sense these pheromones. Males can smell a female up to 1 mile (1.6 km) away when she releases her pheromone.

Some mammals leave smelly messages by spraying urine or leaving dung. Others have special glands that produce a smelly substance. Some deer and antelope have a gland in front of their eye. Some members of the dog, weasel, and mongoose families have their scent glands under the tail. These smells are used to give information to other members of their species. They mark territories and send out sex signals.

Did You Know?

A snake flicks its tongue in and out to taste chemicals in the air. A special organ at the back of the throat, Jacobson's organ, picks up the chemicals from the tongue. This organ helps the snake find out about what's going on in its environment.

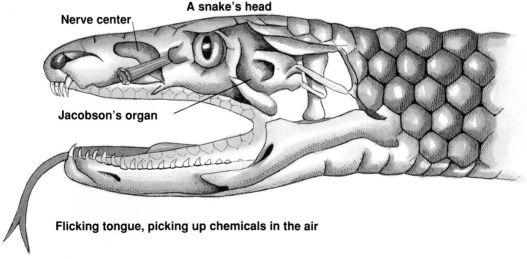

A snake's head

Nerve center

Jacobson's organ

Flicking tongue, picking up chemicals in the air

Hearing and Touch

A bush baby is all ears and eyes. It uses these senses to sense food — and danger. ▶

Bad vibrations

Amphibians, lizards, and birds have no ear flaps at all. Snakes do not even have ears. They are deaf, but they can feel vibrations. So why does a rattlesnake rattle its tail if it cannot hear? Because the rattling warns other animals that can hear to keep their distance. ▼

Did You Know? ▶

Crickets have their ears on their legs. Cicadas have their ears at the base of their wings.

Hearing is important

Hearing is an important sense for animals. Many birds, mammals, and even fish have good hearing. Nocturnal animals and animals living in forests cannot easily see their prey or their enemies among the trees or at night, so they need good hearing.

Most mammals have outer ear flaps, or pinnae, that catch sounds very well. Bush babies and many rodents flick their pinnae all the time searching for sounds.

Seals and crocodiles live both on land and in water. Because they lead an amphibious life, "water flaps" close off their ears. Some desert lizards have a fleshy "comb" stretching out from each ear that stops sand from getting into their ears.

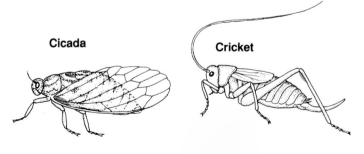

Cicada　　**Cricket**

Area of body used for hearing

Sensitive skin

There are touch receptors all over the surface of our bodies, so most of our skin is sensitive to touch. Our fingertips and tongue are packed with touch receptors, so these parts are more sensitive than parts of our bodies that have fewer touch receptors.

The whiskers on the faces of some mammals are also organs of touch. Cats, mice, and rats use their whiskers to find their way in the dark. Otters and sea lions search for food with theirs.

Snails and slugs have feelers at the front of their heads that quickly shorten if touched. The snail or slug then draws into its shell for protection. Insects, lobsters, and crabs also have feelers, called antennae, that they rely on to find out what's going on in the world around them.

These animals live close to or on the seabed. The gurnard uses one pair of front fins as feelers and searches for small animals buried in the sandy bed of the sea to eat. The catfish has long feelers, called barbels, on its head with which it finds its way in the dark, murky water. It also uses them to detect food. Crabs and lobsters have antennae that they use in a similar way.

▼

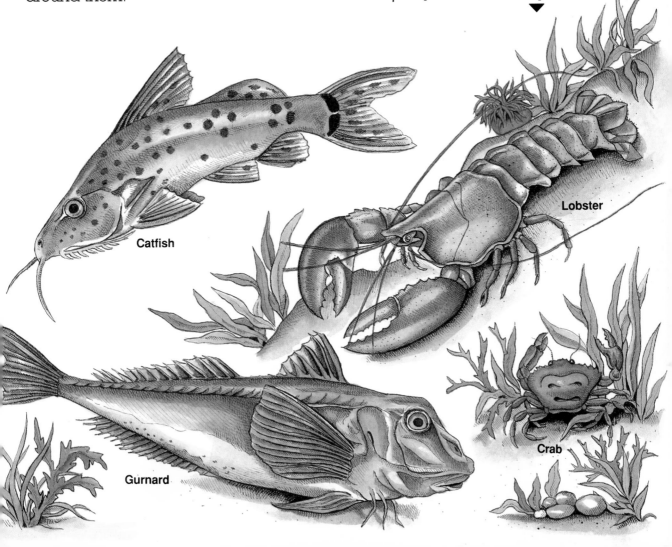

Catfish

Lobster

Gurnard

Crab

The Sixth Sense

The five human senses — vision, hearing, touch, smell, and taste — are not the only senses animals have. Many animals have other ways of finding out about their world.

Shocking senses

Some animals, especially fish, use electricity to find out what is going on around them. The electric eel can produce up to 650 volts. This is more than five times as much as the voltage from a home electric socket. The electric eel lives in the muddy, murky waters of the Amazon River. It finds its way in the water by using electricity like radar. The electric "radar" helps the eel sense what is going on. If a fish swims near the eel this "radar" detects it. It can catch the fish by stunning it with a sudden jolt of electric current.

Lateral line (magnified)

Tiny hairs (pick up movement in the water)

Good vibrations ▲

Fish and some amphibians have a lateral line running down each side of their bodies. The line is like a long row of tiny cups joined up. In the middle of each cup is a tiny hair surrounded by sticky slime, or mucus. These hairs move when there are vibrations in the water. Ducks, other fish, and people on a riverbank all make vibrations that tell the animal what's going on.

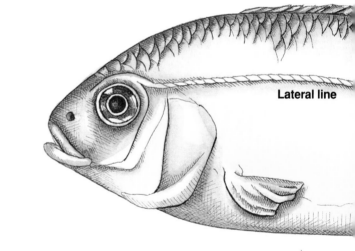

Lateral line

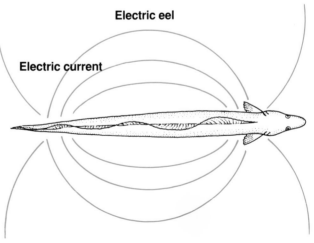

Electric eel

Electric current

The electric eel lives in the murky Amazon River. It gives off a powerful current of electricity around its body, which can be used for defense or attack. ▶

42

This snake is called a Pope's pit viper. There are several different kinds of pit viper, all of which have heat-sensitive pits between each eye and nostril. This enables them to pick up changes in temperature around them. They can sense the heat given off by a small animal, for instance, and know that a tasty meal is close by.

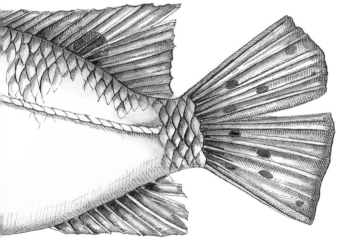

Seeing by hearing

Bats and dolphins use echolocation — another kind of hearing. A bat makes a burst of sharp, high-pitched sound that bounces off objects and back to the bat's ears. The bat can tell where things are, even when it cannot see them. Echolocation helps animals find their way around and find food. It is important for nocturnal animals or animals with poor eyesight, like dolphins.

▼

Heat sensors

The bushmaster of South America and the rattlesnakes of North and South America belong to a group of snakes called pit vipers. Their name comes from heat-sensitive pits between each eye and nostril. The temperature receptors here can pick up such small changes in temperature that a snake can tell if a mouse walks near it from the heat of the mouse's body. Most pit vipers come out at night. The pits help them find prey in the dark.

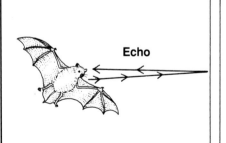

Echo

5: | REPRODUCTION

How Animals Reproduce

Amoebas — Single-celled Creatures

Nucleus

One amoeba

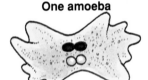

Two nuclei

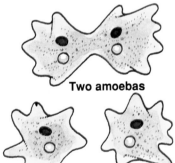

Two amoebas

▲ This diagram shows how an amoeba divides to form two separate living organisms.

The sperm from a human male makes contact with the egg inside the female. This sperm fertilizes the egg and leads to the growth of a baby inside the female.

All animals eventually die. But a species will continue if its members reproduce. Single-celled animals, or protozoans, reproduce by splitting. An amoeba divides down the middle to become two new cells. The hydra, a simple many-celled animal, reproduces by budding off parts of its body. But animals made up of many cells have tissues and organs too complicated to split or bud. They reproduce sexually.

Sexual reproduction

Most animals make sex cells. The males' sex cells are called sperm. The females' sex cell is called the egg. When a sperm pushes into the egg, fertilization takes place. At fertilization, a new living cell is formed. This new cell then grows by dividing up and making many new cells. Eventually these cells form a complete, new animal.

External and internal fertilization

Animals living in water, such as sea anemones, starfish, and most fish and frogs, release millions of sperm and many eggs into the water. So fertilization takes place outside these animals' bodies.

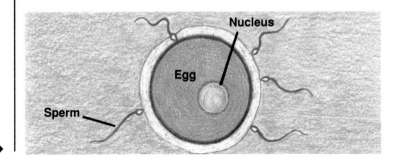

Nucleus

Egg

Sperm

For most land animals, the male uses a sex organ, the penis, to insert sperm into a special opening in the female. Sperm fertilize the eggs inside the female. With internal fertilization, sperm and egg are more likely to meet, so fewer sex cells are needed.

Eggs and young

Some land animals, including some reptiles and all birds, lay eggs. As the young animal or embryo develops inside the shell, it uses its own food supply — the yolk; and when its development is complete it hatches out. Some lizard and snake mothers keep the eggs in their bodies, and their young are born, not hatched. With mammals, the embryo stays inside its mother and gets its food from the mother's blood supply. Mother and embryo are connected by the umbilical cord and placenta. When the embryo has finished developing, the mother gives birth to the young animal.

Facts & Feats

- Male emperor penguins keep, or incubate, their single egg between their feet for safety.

- Only eight weeks after birth, a baby panda weighs 20 times its birth weight.

- A kangaroo's gestation period is only about 34 days. The baby develops in its mother's pouch.

- The gestation period of an elephant is 22 months.

- Many snails are both male and female. An animal like this is a hermaphrodite.

- Male sharks and rays have claspers, specially adapted fins used like a penis for mating with female sharks.

- The duck-billed platypus and the echidna are the only mammals that lay eggs. Like other mammals, they feed their young with milk.

◀ This male and female lion are mating. Fertilization will take place in the lioness's womb and she will carry the developing cub inside her until ready to give birth to her live young.

Finding a Mate

A male peacock fans his magnificent feathers. The display will attract a female, or peahen, and courtship and mating will then take place. ▼

Most animals must find a mate before they can breed. Courtship is an important way to make sure that a male and female of the same species get together and mate. Mating between different species is a waste of time. In general, no fertile young can come from two different species.

Showing off

Many birds, reptiles, amphibians, and fish use bright colors to attract a mate. The male peacock's beautiful feathers form a shimmering fan of color. He uses this to display in front of the peahen (the female), which chooses the peacock with the finest, most colorful plumage. Fine feathers tell the female that the peacock is healthy and strong. By mating with him she will produce healthy young. The male green lizard's throat turns blue in the breeding season. He bobs his head up and down to show the female his throat. If she is interested in him, he grabs her by the base of the tail. Instead of running she moves her front feet in a jerky movement. They are ready to mate.

Dancing delights

Male cocks-of-the-rock clear away forest vegetation so they can gather and dance. Females watch from the trees and choose a mate they like the best.

Both male and female cranes dance as part of their courtship. The male scorpion leads his female partner in the dance. Grabbing her by her pincers, he leads her over a pocket of his sperm he has left in the ground, which she then picks up.

Animal flashlights

Both male and female fireflies flash their lights to attract each other. Deep-sea fish also use lights to attract each other's attention. One species recognizes another by the way their lights flash.

Joined for life

The deep-sea anglerfish has unusual mating habits. The male finds it so difficult to find a mate that when he does he attaches himself to her. Eventually their blood systems join. The food she eats feeds him. He loses his fins and never leaves her.

Different animals attract a partner in different ways. The male scorpion leads the female in a sort of courtship dance. The male crested newt dresses up in bright colors in the breeding season to attract a female. And the male green lizard's throat turns bright blue. ▼

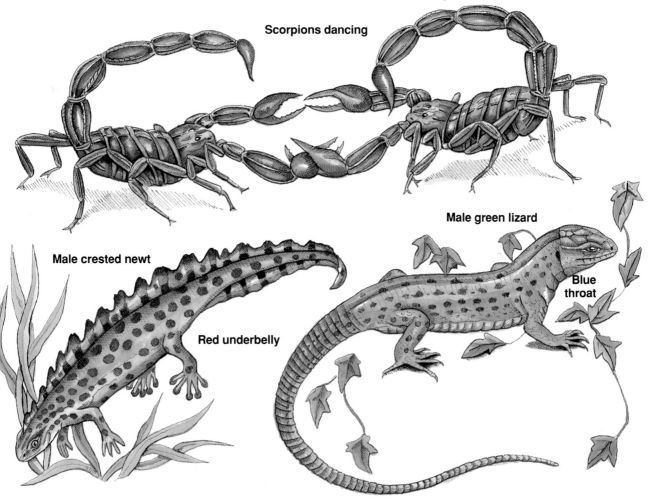

Scorpions dancing

Male green lizard

Blue throat

Male crested newt

Red underbelly

Animal Parents

The female orangutan spends a great amount of time bringing up her single baby. She will protect it and teach it how to survive on its own. ▶

The male midwife toad carries his eggs wrapped around his back legs. In this manner, he will keep them moist and safe from predators. ▼

Once courtship and mating are over, many animals show no further interest in their offspring. The cod produces millions of eggs, but many eggs and young will be eaten, so only a few cod from those millions of eggs will live to be parents themselves.

Other animals take a lot of care in bringing up their young. An orangutan brings up just one baby at a time. But it cares for it, feeds it, and teaches it to survive. Like humans, scorpions, some fish, crocodiles, and many other animals, orangutans show parental care.

Egg protectors

Unlike cod, some animals protect their eggs. They lay fewer eggs, but since the eggs are protected, more young survive. The female giant water bug lays her eggs on the male's back. He carries them everywhere he goes. A female shore crab hides her eggs under her body. A flap of hard shell protects them. The male midwife toad wraps strings of eggs around his legs and keeps them moist and safe. A female wolf spider carries her silk cocoon of eggs around with her.

This female kangaroo carries her young in a pouch. The baby is born very small and helpless and crawls into her pouch, where it stays until it is better able to look after itself. Kangaroos are marsupials. This means they have a pouch for carrying their young. Other types of marsupial are wombats, bandicoots, and opossums.

Birds and mammals

Some young birds and mammals can look after themselves soon after they are born. Soon after hatching, pheasants and chickens start looking for food. Antelope and deer follow the herd only hours after being born.

All mammals feed their young milk. As the young one grows up, the mother will refuse to give it milk, but helps it eat solid food. This is called weaning. The mother koala weans its young on partly digested leaves. The mother produces this special food as dung. Eventually, the baby koala will eat leaves straight from the tree. This is all part of how the baby animal grows up to become an adult.

The female Nile crocodile carries her newly hatched young in a very strange place. She puts them in her mouth for safety.

Bringing up babies

Some cichlid fish seem to eat their young. But the parents really only take the young into their mouths for protection. This is called mouth-brooding. The Nile crocodile carries her newly hatched young in a pouch in her mouth.

Changing

Dragonfly and mayfly larvae hatch from eggs laid in water (for instance, pond water). As they grow, they shed their old skins until finally they develop into the adult and fly away.
▼

Some animals look very different from their parents when they are young. Crabs, for instance, start life as an egg and then grow into a larva. They only start to look like crabs when they grow out of the larval form. This change in development is called metamorphosis.

Adult mussels and barnacles often attach themselves to rocks and ships. But their microscopic larvae float in the water and become part of the plankton. They have strange shapes, with long, feathery parts that keep them afloat. Ocean currents carry the larvae miles from their parents, so parents and their young do not compete for the same space and food. Drifting larvae help spread the species around the world.

Twisting and turning

A newly hatched flounder looks like most other larval fish. But after several days, the eye on one side of its head slowly moves until it ends up next to the eye on the other side. After this, the fish flips over onto one side, so both eyes look up. For the rest of its life it swims along the seabed on its side.

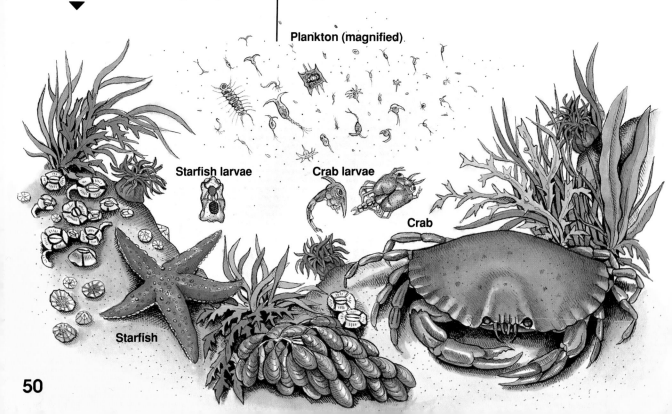

Plankton (magnified).

Starfish larvae

Crab larvae

Crab

Starfish

Adult frog

Eggs (or spawn)

Froglet with a tail

Tadpole

Tadpole with hind legs

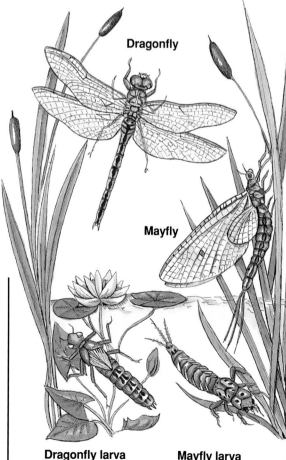

Dragonfly

Mayfly

Dragonfly larva   **Mayfly larva**

A different world

Dragonflies, mayflies, and mosquitoes never compete with their young. They all lay their eggs in water, and the larvae live in water feeding and growing. To grow, they must shed their old skins. Eventually they shed their last pupal skin and change into an adult. Since adult mayflies live for only about a day or two, female mayflies must find a mate and lay their eggs very quickly.

6: | ANIMAL COMMUNITIES

Living Together

Not all animals live together in groups, or colonies. An example of a solitary animal is the tiger. A tiger usually hunts and feeds alone in its own territory with enough food in it to keep alive, and it chases other tigers away. Tigers usually come together only during the breeding season to mate, and the female tiger will spend time rearing her cubs. But most animals do live with others of their kind for part or all of their lives.

Starlings feed in flocks. At night, many of these flocks join together to make one huge flock of hundreds of starlings. These starlings all roost together at night.

Living together in the open in groups helps animals stay safe from attack. One antelope is much safer in a herd than on its own. With more eyes, ears, and noses around to sense danger, the chance of one antelope being caught is far smaller in a herd. Also, there are so many other antelope around for a predator to attack.

This pack of wolves lives, breeds, hunts, and rears its young together. Being in a pack helps them survive. They can work together to get food, and each wolf can watch out for signs of danger to the pack.

Sharing for survival

Some predators live in groups also. Wolves live in packs and help each other catch and kill their prey. One wolf on its own is not strong enough to kill a moose, but a pack of wolves working together can. Members of the pack share their kill among themselves. In short, the wolves cooperate with each other to make sure they get their food.

Breeding groups

Northern elephant seals spend most of their lives out at sea. Nobody knows exactly where they go or how they live. But they return to breed on beaches in Mexico and California. Here they form breeding groups. Males fight over females, and the strongest ones mate with the females. Once the females have their calves, they return to sea.

Like elephant seals, male deer fight over females. Once the breeding season is over, some of the males go off and form "stag parties," or herds. The females and young live in separate groups with a single male.

▲ On the African plains live herds of different animals, such as impalas (a type of antelope), wildebeests, and zebras. A herd works on the principle that there is safety in numbers.

These female northern elephant seals make up part of a larger breeding group. ▼

Animal Colonies

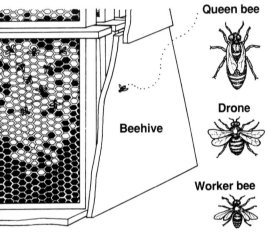

Queen bee

Drone

Beehive

Worker bee

▲ Bees live in a hive. There are three main types: the queen bee, the male drones, and sterile female worker bees.

Baboons are social animals. They live together in a well-ordered group with a dominant male who, with the help of younger males, protects them from attacks. The baboons groom each other. This strengthens the closeness of the group. ▶

Some animals live very close together. They depend on each other for survival. There are many examples of this cooperation throughout the animal kingdom.

Naked mole rats

The naked mole rat of Africa lives in colonies with a queen. She stays queen by producing a chemical in her urine that stops the other females from reproducing. Naked mole rats tunnel underground to find the roots and tubers of plants to eat. As they tunnel, they form a long line. The one at the front passes the earth back to the one behind, and so on. The one at the back kicks it out of the entrance. If a snake attacks the burrow, the one at the end squeaks a warning to the others. They fill up the entrance to protect themselves. But the one at the end will probably be eaten by the snake. It gives up its life to help the others. Some naked mole rats act like soldiers protecting the colony from attack. The survival of the colony is more important than any one individual.

Queens in control

Bees, wasps, and ants live in colonies, also ruled by a queen. There are three kinds of bee in a honeybee colony: the female queen, who lays the eggs and controls the colony; the male drones, whose only job is to mate with new queens; and the workers (females who cannot reproduce but collect food, feed the colony, and rear the young).

Some ant colonies have soldier ants, as well as workers, drones, and a queen. Soldier ants fight to the death in defending their colony. They have huge jaws or stings to frighten off any attackers.

Coral colonies

Corals are made up of many tiny animals that together form a colony. Each animal is called a polyp. Each polyp looks like a miniature sea anemone. All these polyps grow from each other and are all connected together. They share food with each other.

◀ This coral colony is made up of thousands of tiny animals called polyps. In their community, the polyps live on top of each other.

The Portuguese Man-of-War

The Portuguese man-of-war is really a colony of many different polyps. Different polyps do different jobs. Some polyps form the tentacles for catching food. Others make up the parts of the animal that reproduce. The float that acts like a sail is one big polyp. Each group of polyps has its own job to do, and it relies on other groups of polyps to help it survive. This is called division of labor.

▼

Animal Partners

In nature, animals depend on each other, whether it's for food when a predator kills and eats its prey, or for reproduction when a male and female of the same species mate. In some partnerships, one species needs another. In some, the species help each other. In others, one can be harmed.

Friends helping friends

Ants and aphids help each other. Aphids make honeydew, a sweet, sugary liquid that ants like to eat. Ants "milk" the aphids, as people milk cows, to get the honeydew. In return, the ants protect the aphids. They fight off the aphids' enemies, such as ladybugs, with their bites and stings.

Some animals depend on plants. Corals depend on tiny plants called algae for their growth. Algae live in the soft parts of the coral polyps and help speed up the growth of the chalky skeletons of corals. Without the algae, corals grow very slowly.

Swimming among the coral reefs of tropical seas are tiny fish called cleaner wrasse. They earn their food by keeping other fish healthy. The cleaner wrasse eat dead skin and small parasites on other fish. Often, large groups of fish gather at cleaning "stations," waiting patiently for their turn to be cleaned. Without the cleaner wrasse, other fish would become ill. Without the fish to clean, the wrasse would be hungry. All these are examples of different species helping each other survive.

Tapeworm

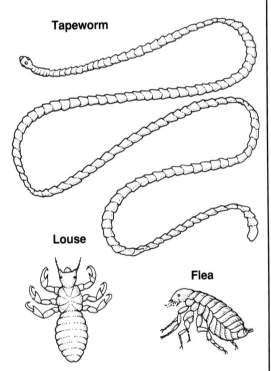

Louse

Flea

▲ These three animals are examples of parasites. They live on or inside another animal and feed off it. They do not kill the host animal, for this would cut off their food supply.

These ants are milking aphids. The ants protect the aphids from their enemies, such as ladybugs. ▶

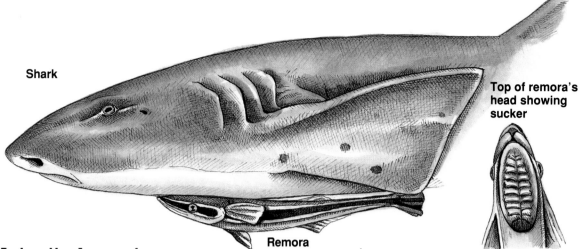

Shark

Remora

Top of remora's head showing sucker

Uninvited guests

In some partnerships, only one member of a pair gains. For example, a species of ragworm lives in the shell of a hermit crab. The crab is the one that finds all the food. While the crab is eating, the ragworm pops out and helps himself to some of the crab's meal. It gives the hermit crab nothing back in return for its free food.

Fish called remoras have a special fin that acts like a sucker. A remora can hitch a free ride on a shark using its sucker fin as it feeds on the shark's scraps and leftovers.

Clownfish hide among the deadly tentacles of giant sea anemones. The anemone's sting kills most fish, but it does not sting clownfish. These fish are safe from danger in the tentacles. They also eat scraps of the anemone's meal, and yet the clownfish do not seem to help the anemone.

Hermit crabs, sharks, and sea anemones gain nothing from their relationships, yet they tolerate their uninvited guests.

▲ The remora is a fish that attaches itself to the underside of a shark. It feeds off of scraps from the shark.

◀ These clownfish hide among the deadly tentacles of a sea anemone. They are safe from attack by predators because the anemone protects them.

Sending Messages

These butterfly fish live in the coral reefs. They are all similarly marked so they can recognize each other. ▶

▲ The white-tail deer flags its tail as a warning of danger.

There are slight differences in the markings on these killer whales. Each killer whale has its own distinct pattern, like fingerprints of a human being. ▼

Talking is a major means of communication for people. Talking helps us find out what is going on around us. Whales and dolphins are among the only other animals that talk to each other. But most animals, especially those in groups, need to communicate. They do this in a variety of ways.

What are you?

The different colors and patterns on animals' bodies help distinguish them from one another. Coral reef fish use their bright colors the way athletic teams use uniforms. Members of the same species can recognize each other and avoid fish of different colors.

Individual animals of the same species vary. They generally look alike, but also have individual markings, just like human fingerprints. Killer whales can be recognized by their slightly different pattern shapes.

In groups of monkeys, the leading male has features that make him look different from the others. Like the male mandrill — who has a bright blue and red face and a backside to match — he can be recognized easily by others in the group as their leader.

Mood signals

Animals can change their moods quickly. When they do, they give off signals. For instance, the cuttlefish changes color when it is excited. Monkeys and apes show their mood by changing their facial expression. A yawn by a male monkey doesn't always mean he is tired. He might be threatening another monkey in the troop by showing off his long teeth. If the other monkey doesn't behave, there can be trouble. One way it can calm the male is to make submissive squeals by smacking its lips. This tells the male that it wants to groom him. Monkeys enjoy grooming and being groomed. The dominant male is groomed by his troop more than he grooms them. In return, he leads the troop and defends it from enemies.

▲The mandrill is a type of baboon from Western Africa. The male has a brightly colored face that marks him as a leader.

Territory

Animals communicate where the boundaries of their territory lie. Birds sing early in the morning. Gibbons shout across the forest. Lizards bob their heads and show off bright colors on their throats. Tomcats spray urine. These signals warn animals not to enter their territory. If they do, they may be attacked.

◄ Spreading the news

Communication is important for an animal that wants to tell something to the rest of its group. Bees tell one another where to find a new supply of food by dancing and wiggling their bottoms. This tells other bees how far away the food is.

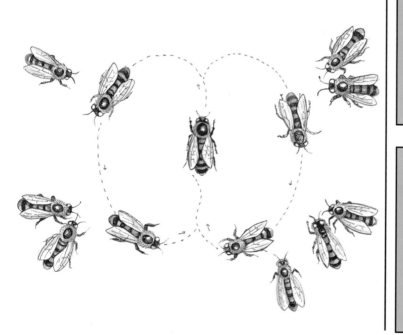

Glossary

Adapted: Suited to live a particular way of life.

Amoeba: A tiny, single-celled animal that changes shape as it moves.

Amphibious animal: An animal that lives in water and on land, such as a frog.

Ancestor: A relative who was alive in the past.

Antennae: Long structures on or near the head of some animals that can be used to touch, taste, and even smell.

Aquatic mammal: A mammal that lives in water, such as a dolphin or a whale.

Baleen: Whalebone; an elastic, hornlike material made from the same material as hair and fingernails that hangs from the top of some whales' mouths and is used for filtering out tiny animals from the water.

Barbels: Fleshy "whiskers" found on some fish that can touch, taste, and smell.

Bower: An area of ground decorated by a male bowerbird to attract a female bowerbird.

Camouflage: The use of colors, patterns, and shapes to help animals stay hidden against a specific background.

Canine teeth: Teeth found in most mammals. They are long and daggerlike in cats and dogs, and short but pointed in humans.

Carbon dioxide: A gas produced when animals breathe. It is formed from carbon and oxygen.

Carnassial teeth: Teeth found in some carnivorous mammals, such as cats and dogs, used for tearing apart meat and bones.

Cicada: An insect with a broad head and transparent wings. The male makes a loud, high-pitched sound.

Clot: To clump together to become more solid than liquid, such as when blood clots to stop a cut from bleeding.

Communication: The exchange of information between two or more individuals.

Compete: In the case of animals, to struggle for limited food, space, and mates.

Compound eye: An eye made up of many smaller simple parts, each with its own lens.

Density: How much something weighs for its size. Water is denser than air because if the same volumes of air and water were weighed, water would weigh much more than air.

Diffusion: The movement of gases or liquids from an area of high concentration to an area of low concentration.

Digestion: The process by which food is broken down into a form that can be taken up into the rest of the body.

Dissolve: To change from a solid or gas into a liquid.

Division of labor: The sharing of work.

Dominant: Of higher standing than another animal of the same habitat.

Echidna: A kind of spiny anteater from Australia and New Guinea.

Echolocation: The ability of an animal to use sound to find its way around.

Egg: The female sex cell.

Embryo: An early stage in the development of an animal, just after the stage of the egg cell.

Energy: The force or power used to move things or do work. There are many kinds of energy, such as heat, light, sound, and chemical and nuclear energy.

Evolve: To change gradually, over long periods of time.

Extinct: In the case of living things, no longer existing in living form.

Fertilization: The joining of male and female sex cells to create a unified cell.

Flatworm: A simple organism found in water.

Focus: A point at which light rays meet to give a clear image of an object.

Fossilization: What happens when the hard parts of dead animals become preserved in rocks.

Generation: Animals born at a similar point in time and so of the same age group.

Genus: A group of closely related animals that contains several species.

Gestation: The length of time from fertilization until birth.

Gills: Parts of the body used by certain water animals, such as fish, for taking oxygen from the water.

Herbivores: Animals that eat only plants or parts of plants such as fruit, seeds, and nectar.

Hermaphrodite: An animal that produces both male and female sex cells.

Hermit crab: A kind of crab that lives in the shell of another animal, like a snail, for protection.

Honeydew: Sugary fluid made by insects.

Hydra: A tiny polyp with a tube-shaped body and a mouth ringed with tentacles.

Incubate: To keep eggs warm for hatching.

Jet propulsion: A way of moving using a backward force to push forward.

Krill: Small shrimplike animals found in such enormous numbers that they are the food of many animals in the ocean, including whales.

Larva: An early stage of some animals' development. It looks different from the adult. Caterpillars and grubs are insect larvae.

Lateral line: A sense organ in fish and some amphibians used to detect vibrations.

Lens: A clear object that is curved to bend light rays passing through it.

Malaria: A disease caused by a single-celled organism called *Plasmodium* which is carried by mosquitoes.

Mandrill: A type of monkey from Africa.

Membrane: A thin layer of material that lines or covers a part of the body.

Metamorphosis: A complete change from the larval form of an animal into the adult form.

Microscopic: Something that is so small it can only be seen with a microscope.

Mouthbrooding: In the case of some animals (mainly fish), protecting eggs and young by keeping them safe in the parents' mouths.

Mucus: Slimy substance produced in or on an animal's body.

Nectar: A sugary liquid made by plants that is high in energy.

Network: An interweaving system.

Nocturnal: A word used to describe animals that are active at night.

Nutritious: In the case of food, rich in goodness and energy.

Olfactory: Concerned with the sense of smell.

Omnivores: Animals that eat both plants and animals.

Oxygen: A gas that nearly all living things breathe. It is found in air and water.

Parasite: A plant or animal living in or on a different kind of plant or animal that gets its food from that plant or animal.

Parental care: Caring behavior shown by parents toward their young.

Pectoral: Having to do with the chest.

Pelvic bone: A bone in the lower part of a vertebrate's body.

Penis: The male sex organ.

Pheromone: A chemical made by an animal which, when released, acts as a signal for another individual of the same species.

Pinna (plural: pinnae): The ear flap of skin found only in mammals.

Plankton: The name given to the many tiny and microscopic plants and animals that drift with the tides and currents in the seas.

Polyp: A tube-shaped animal with a ring of tentacles around its mouth.

Predator: Any animal that kills other animals for food, such as a lion.

Prehensile: Adapted for gripping or holding, like a spider monkey's tail.

Prey: Any animal that becomes the food of another, like an antelope eaten by a lion.

Proboscis: In some animals, the long part of a mouth used in feeding, such as a butterfly's sucking organ or an elephant's trunk.

Protozoan: A primitive, single-celled animal.

Pupil: Opening in the front of the eye through which light enters.

Rabies: A deadly disease passed from animal to animal by biting.

Radar: A device for finding the distance and measuring the speed of a distant object by bouncing radio waves off it.

Ragworm: A kind of worm that lives in the mud and sand of the seashore.

Recycle: To treat substances or materials that have been thrown away, such as newspapers, glass, or cans, so they can be used again.

Remora: A fish that has a special sucker on its head for attaching itself to sharks and other animals.

Reproduction: The process of making new individuals of a species.

Retina: A light-sensitive layer of cells at the back of the eye.

Roost: A place where birds rest.

Ruminate: To regurgitate food and chew it for a second time.

Saliva: A liquid substance made in the mouth of mammals that helps digestion.

Savanna: A kind of open grassland found in Africa, home to giraffes, antelope, lions, and many other African animals.

Scavengers: Animals that eat dead or rotting plant and animal life.

Sheath: A thin outer covering that surrounds and protects.

Solitary: Living alone.

Species: A group of animals so closely related that they can breed with each other.

Sperm: Male sex cells.

Spiracles: The holes in the sides of an insect's body used for breathing.

Streamlined: Curved in order to move easily through water or air.

Temperature receptor: A tiny sense organ lying in the skin of animals that reacts to temperature.

Territory: An area where an animal or group of animals lives which they will defend as their own against other members of the same species.

Touch receptor: A tiny sense organ lying in the skin of animals that reacts to being touched.

Tuber: An underground stem swollen with food.

Umbilical cord: In certain animals, the flexible, cordlike structure connecting the developing young to its mother.

Urine: Fluid made by animals to remove waste products from the body.

Venom: A special poisonous liquid used by many different animals to kill their prey or defend themselves from attackers.

Vibrations: Quick, continuous backward and forward movements.

Warning colors: The bright colors on certain poisonous animals that warn other animals that they are dangerous.

Weaning: The time of change in a young mammal's diet from its mother's milk to adult food.

Womb: The uterus; the place where a young mammal grows inside its mother.

Index

A **boldface** number shows that the entry is illustrated on that page. The same page often has text about the entry, too.